A Celebration of Black History through Music

from spirituals to hip-hop

by Blair Bielawski

Editor: Barbara S. Meeks
Cover and book design: Digital Dynamite, Inc.

Photo credits:
Chuck Berry, © www.VoteJoeC.com
James Brown, © kainita
Miles Davis, © tompalumbo
Aretha Franklin, © Personeelsnet
http://www.flickr.com
http://creativecommons.org/licenses/by-sa/2.0

Printed in the United States of America

ISBN 978-1-4291-1503-2

P.O. Box 802 • Dayton, OH 45401
www.LorenzEducationalPress.com

Nelson

Table of Contents

How to Use This Book

The goal of *A Celebration of Black History through Music...from spirituals to hip-hop* is to introduce your students to the rich history of African-American music and to demonstrate how this music has influenced and shaped the music of the world. This book features some of the most important musicians of each style of music covered, and highlights how the roots of African-American music can be traced from the slave songs of the 1700s through hip-hop music of the 1970s and 80s.

The CD that accompanies this book is an integral part of the experience. It has been said that the history of a people is found in its songs. Obviously, words alone will not do justice to any of the music described in this book—your students must HEAR it. We have done our best to use authentic recordings wherever possible; however, copyright restrictions prohibited the use of some of the original music. In these cases, we created music that is an accurate representation of the style, and provided information of where to find the original source material. We've also included a discography that features available CDs in the event you would like to study this wealth of music in more detail.

As with any timeline regarding music (or any of the arts) the "starting" and "ending" dates for each era are somewhat arbitrary. Impress upon your students the fact that none of the musical styles in this book have disappeared. Music, and all the arts, continues to grow and evolve while keeping alive the traditions of earlier decades and centuries.

Special Features

The appendix of this book includes many reproducible worksheets, extension activities and a printed version of the complete PowerPoint presentation that is included on the enhanced CD. We encourage you to go over the *Vocabulary Word Bank* with your students before you begin teaching the other material in the book. The Word Bank includes some "music-specific" words that they might not know. The reproducible worksheets are designed to be used at the completion of the entire unit, but you might want to use them along the way as a "pre-test".

> *The PowerPoint presentation included on the enhanced CD takes you through the entire book one step at a time, and when used in conjunction with the audio portion of the CD gives a complete picture of the material covered. We highly encourage you to use this resource.*

Vocabulary Word Bank

A cappella Singing without instrumental accompaniment. *The choir sang a cappella.*

Accompaniment A vocal or instrumental part that supports another part. *The piano provided accompaniment for the solo singer.*

Album Before CDs, iTunes and mp3 players, music was recorded on vinyl, and was referred to as an album. *The Miles Davis album called* Kind of Blue *sold more than 500,000 copies.*

Arrangement In music, an arrangement means there are specific, written out parts for each performer. *The composer wrote an arrangement of the song* Autumn Leaves *for the band.*

Art Song A vocal music composition for solo singer and piano intended for recital or other "formal" performance. *She sang a Franz Schubert art song at the concert.*

Backbeat When a piece of music is accented on beats 2 and 4. *The drummer on that rock and roll song is playing a strong backbeat.*

Bebop A type of jazz music started in the late 1940s that is characterized by fast tempos and difficult melodies. *Charlie Parker was an important force in the development of bebop and jazz.*

Blues A sad or mournful kind of song with a specific lyric structure and form. Saint Louis Blues *by W.C. Handy is a famous blues chart.*

Big Band Ensembles of 12–18 musicians (including saxophones, trumpets, trombones and a rhythm section) that play written out jazz swing arrangements. *In the 1920s and 30s, Duke Ellington led his own big band.*

Break-beats Percussive sections of songs played back-to-back on multiple turntables. *The break-beat style is extremely popular in clubs and dance halls because break dancers can use it to show their skills.*

Carnegie Hall Built in New York City in 1891 (and refurbished in 1986), this performance space is recognized the world over as one of the ultimate places to hear serious music. *Sharon got to hear the New York Philharmonic Orchestra perform at Carnegie Hall.*

Chords A musical term, a chord is three or more different notes played at the same time. *There are hundreds of chords that may be played on the piano.* A "chord progression" describes how chords change during a piece of music. *The blues has a specific chord progression.*

Classical Music This refers to all "serious" music in the Western European tradition. *Jennifer and James went to hear an orchestra play a classical music concert.*

Dixieland A style of jazz which developed in New Orleans at the beginning of the 20th century. *A well-known jazz standard song from the Dixieland era is* Washington and Lee Swing.

DJ (Deejay or Disc Jockey) The person who selects music and runs turntables in a dance club. *Hip-hop DJs use turntable scratching to create percussive sounds.*

Emancipation Proclamation This consists of two executive orders issued by President Lincoln during the American Civil War. The first order declared the freedom of all slaves in the Confederate States of America that did not return to the Union by the year 1863. The second order listed the specific states where the proclamation applied.

Genre A type, class or style of art, music, literature, etc. *Dixieland music is one of the parts of the jazz genre.*

Gospel Music Music that combines Christian praise with the harmony and rhythms of the blues. *Thomas Dorsey is known as the "Father of Gospel Music."*

Head Charts The compositions performed by bebop players who memorized the melody and chords to each song and would simply improvise the rest. *Blair was a great head chart player because he was so good at improvising.*

Hip-hop A musical genre which began in the Bronx in the 1970s typically consisting of a rhythmic vocal style called 'rap' accompanied by backbeats. *Kool Herc is one of the three men credited with starting the hip-hop genre in New York.*

Hymn A type of song written for the purpose of prayer or praise. *Slaves related to the message of the hymns written by Isaac Watts; many of which are still sung in churches today.*

Improvise (improvisation) Composing music spontaneously or "on the spot". Playing or singing music with nothing notated. *Jazz musicians need to know how to improvise.*

MC (emcee or MJ—microphone jockey) The host of an event or performance. *The MC usually introduces performers, speaks to the audience, and keeps the event moving. An MC delivers rhymes and dialog in the rhythm of the music he is playing.*

Measure A short segment of music. A composition is divided into measures. If a paragraph is a musical composition, the words in the paragraph are the measures. *The song is 32 measures long.* "Bar" is another word for measure.

Melody The most prominent part of a song or instrumental piece. *Suzanne sang the melody of the song.*

New York City One of the most important cities in the development of African-American music like jazz and hip-hop. It is divided into five areas called "boroughs": Brooklyn, The Bronx, Staten Island, Harlem and Queens. *Hip-hop music was developed in the Bronx.*

Ragtime An American musical genre popular between 1897 and 1918. It began as dance music in American cities such as St. Louis and New Orleans. *Scott Joplin is known as the "Father of ragtime."*

Repertoire A collection of music pieces played by an individual musician or group, or composed for a particular instrument or group of instruments. *Many of Duke Ellington's works have become standards in jazz repertoire.*

Rock and Roll (often written as rock & roll or rock 'n' roll) A genre of popular music that evolved in the United States in the late 1940s and early 1950s. Its roots lay mainly in blues, rhythm and blues, country, folk, gospel, and jazz. *The television show, American Bandstand, brought the top rock and roll groups into the homes of teenagers.*

Scratching A DJ technique used to produce distinctive sounds by moving a vinyl record back and forth on a turntable. *Hip-hop DJs invented scratching techniques in the 1980s.*

Secular Non-sacred, non-religious. Take Me Out To the Ballgame *is a secular song.*

Shout A performance after a church service that happened in an open area and involved soloists "shouting" out praises and urging the group on with their singing and chanting.

Solo One featured singer or instrumentalist. *Natalia sang a solo with the choir.* "Solo" may also refer to a section of improvised music in jazz. *Louis played a great solo in that piece.*

Soul Music A music genre originating in the United States that combined elements of gospel music with rhythm and blues. *James Brown is referred to as the "Godfather of Soul."*

Spiritual Religious folk songs created and first sung by enslaved African-Americans. Swing Low, Sweet Chariot *is one of the most famous spirituals.*

Syncopation Putting stress or "accenting" a typically weak beat in music. "Syncopation" is often used in jazz to give it a "swing" feel. *Dixieland music uses more syncopation than classical music.*

Tempo The speed of a piece of music. *The slow tempo of the song made it sound sad.*

Work Song Music that portrayed the living and working conditions that slaves were forced to endure—sung by people working on physical or competitive tasks and used to regulate the pace of their work.

Chapter 1: Roots

Beginning in 1619, and for more than 200 years after that, Africans were forcibly removed from their homes and families and shipped across the Atlantic Ocean to North and South America to be sold into slavery. Many of these Africans ended up working on plantations in the Southern states of America. Music was then, and is to this day, an integral part of life in Africa, so it was natural that the men and women brought there would use singing as a way to communicate their feelings.

The Old Plantation. **Artist unknown, c. 1790-1800.**

Work Songs, Hymns and Shouts

By the mid-1700s several different kinds of songs had evolved. One of the types of songs that grew from this period is called a "work song." This music portrays the living and working conditions that slaves were forced to endure. These were songs sung by people working on physical and repetitive tasks like harvesting crops, laying railroad tracks or hammering steel. They used these songs to regulate the pace of their work, and sometimes to comment on their masters using improvised "coded" lyrics. A work song was also sung to help alleviate the boredom and stress of these monotonous tasks.

Hoe Emma, Hoe

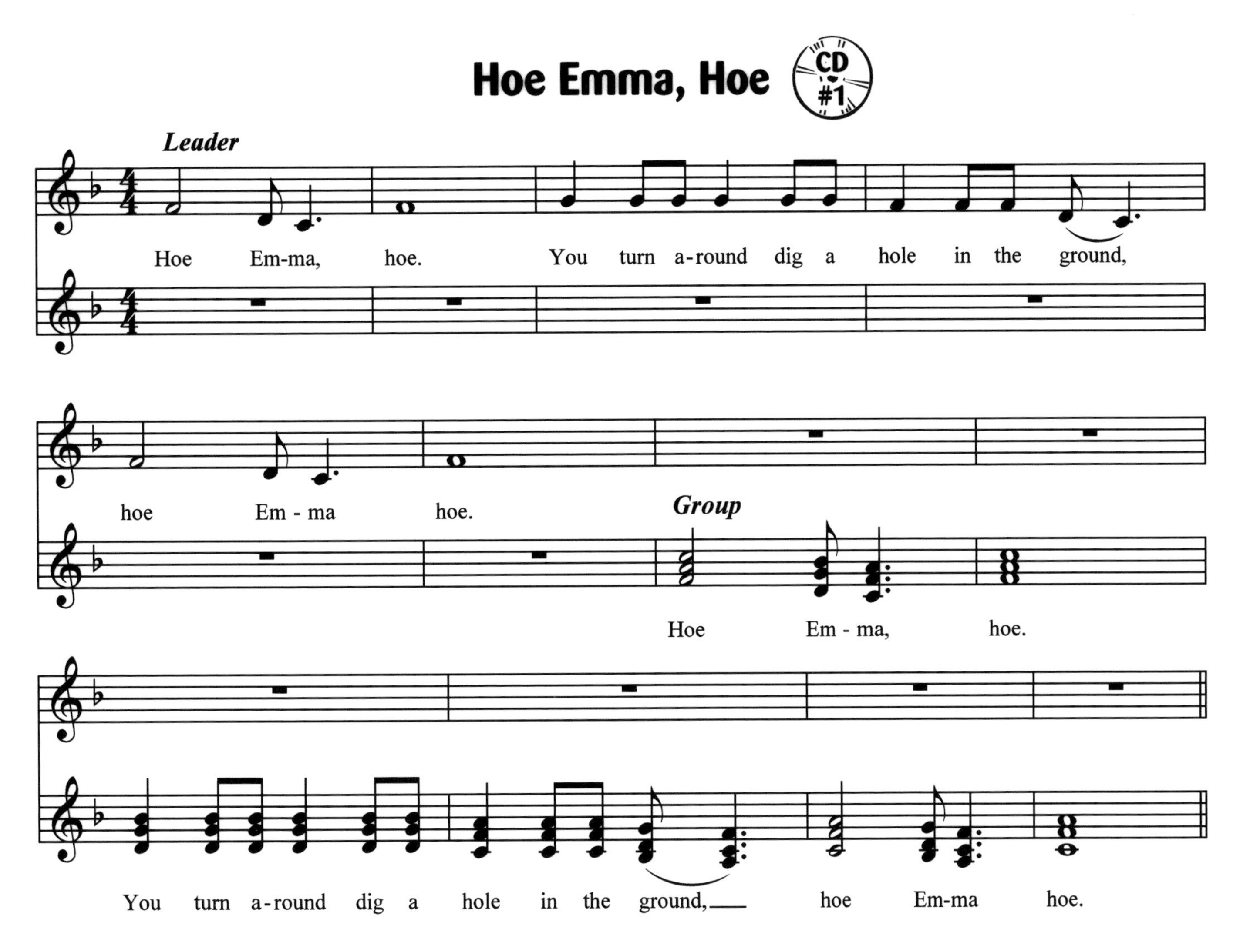

Another kind of song that became important to slaves during this time was the "hymn." The only place that slaves were allowed to meet outside of work was at church, so songs they found in hymnals of the time often became important to them and were assimilated into their culture. Strangely enough, the hymn composer whose words meant the most to slaves was a white, English composer named Isaac Watts. He was brought up as a "Nonconformist" or "dissenter"—someone who believes in God, but was not part of the religious community that was recognized by the Church of England.

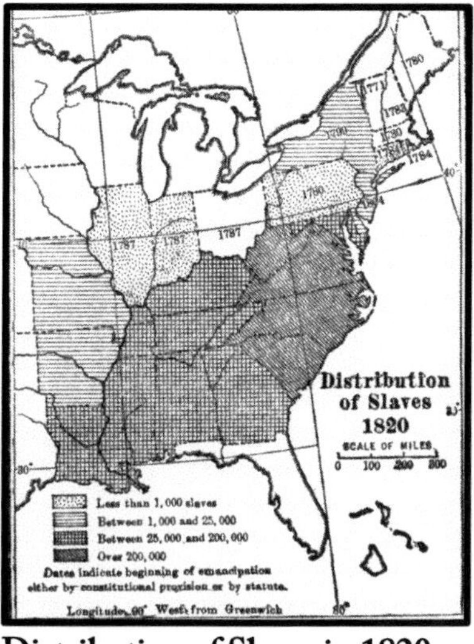

Distribution of Slaves in 1820

This is probably why the slaves were able to relate to the message of the hymns of Watts…his words reached out to their emotions and helped connect the singer more personally to the text than "traditional" psalms of the church had in the past. Many hymns by Isaac Watts are still sung today. For example, the Christmas song *Joy to the World* was written by Watts as was *O God, Our Help in Ages Past* and *When I Survey the Wondrous Cross.*

A special dance and song that took place after the regular church service was over was another kind of music that developed during this time. Called a "shout", this performance was done in an open area and involved a soloist or small ensemble singing while everyone else joined hands and moved in a circle. Eventually, the song would turn into a chant with soloists "shouting" out praises and urging the group on with their singing and chanting.

Spirituals

By 1830 or so, attempts were made to notate the improvised songs of the slaves. The first collection of "plantation songs" was finally published in 1867 and included shouts and work songs along with the most important genre of African-American music from this period: the *spiritual.* Spirituals grew from a combination of shouts, chants, work songs and the specific religious experience of Africans in America who were converted to Christianity. Spirituals are religious folk songs created and first sung by African-Americans in slavery.

Some of the most famous spirituals are:

- *Swing Low, Sweet Chariot*
- *Joshua Fit the Battle of Jericho*
- *Sometimes I Feel Like a Motherless Child*
- *Go Down, Moses*
- *Wade in the Water*

In the years since 1867, music historians and scholars have documented thousands of spirituals, and in 1998 it was reported that the Library of Congress had more than six thousand spirituals on record. The majority of these songs can be classified into three groups:

1. Call and response
2. Slow, long-phrase melody
3. Syncopated, segmented melody

Classification of Spirituals

In the “call and response” spiritual a song leader sings a line and the rest of the group responds with a refrain that stays constant throughout the rest of the song. The majority of these songs are fast and intense. *Sittin’ Down Beside O’ the Lamb* is a good example of the call and response spiritual.

Sittin’ Down Beside O’ the Lamb

Swing Low, Sweet Chariot, one of the best known spirituals of all time, is in the call and response form.

Swing Low, Sweet Chariot

The second classification of the spiritual, the slow, long-phrased melody, is less common than the call and response form, but includes some very famous spirituals like *Deep River* and *Nobody Knows the Trouble I've Seen.* The lyrics in these songs usually longer, more complete sentences than in the other forms of spirituals. Instead of the short, segmented melodic fragments in call and response, the melodies in this style are long and flowing to better match the text.

The third type of spiritual features a segmented, syncopated melody. (*Syncopation* is a rhythmic technique that places stress on beats that are usually weak. It's like accenting the wrong syllable of a word.) Well-known songs in this category are *Little David, Play Your Harp, Down by the Riverside* and the example below.

Gonna Shout All Over God's Heaven

In 1863, President Lincoln signed the Emancipation Proclamation which freed slaves in Confederate-controlled areas of the Southern United States. In 1864, the United States Senate ratified the 13th Amendment to the Constitution which abolished slavery throughout the country. It is possible that the legacy of the Negro spiritual might have died away with the end of slavery…many of the freed men and women wanted to forget the past and move on with their lives. However, in 1867, a new institution was founded that would take the traditional spiritual across the country and into Europe to establish its rightful place in music history.

Fisk University and the Jubilee Singers

Just six months after the end of the Civil War, Fisk University was founded in Nashville, Tennessee. The goal of the new college was to provide African-Americans with the best education available in the United States. The school had financial trouble in its first few years of operation so the "Jubilee Singers" was formed in the hope that they could take their music to people across the country and raise enough money to keep Fisk University open. Their first tour began in 1871 and ended up being such a success that they raised enough money to preserve the university and build the first permanent structure for the education of black students—Jubilee Hall.

Over the course of time, American composers began to use spirituals as the basis for new choral compositions based on Western European traditions of "art songs"—songs intended for serious performance in concert halls. These new pieces helped to elevate the spiritual to its rightful place in American history and in world music history. The following arrangement of *I Couldn't Hear Nobody Pray* by André Thomas demonstrates the use of a spiritual in a contemporary choral setting.

I Couldn't Hear Nobody Pray

The Blues

During the development of the spiritual as the main sacred music of the African-American in the late 1800s and early 1900s, another kind of music was emerging as the main secular (non-church) style of music: the blues. The term "blues" is often used to refer to any sad or mournful kind of song, but it actually describes a very specific kind of lyric structure and form. A blues has three lines of lyrics in each stanza. The first line and the second line are the same while the third line provides an answer or comment on the first two lines. For example, here is the first stanza of the W.C. Handy composition *Saint Louis Blues*:

I hate to see the evening sun go down.

I hate to see the evening sun go down.

'Cause my baby she done left this town.

St. Louis Blues

The blues form also has a specific music form. The basic blues is 12 measures long with a simple, repetitive chord sequence.

Blues Sequence

Like spirituals, the earliest blues songs were probably sung a cappella (with no instrumental accompaniment). As the style evolved, it became common for the singer to accompany themselves on guitar. As we will see throughout the development of African-American music, New Orleans and other "Delta" areas of the South were the birthplace of several styles of music, and this was certainly the case with the blues.

Robert Johnson

Singer and guitarist Robert Johnson (1911–1938) is one of the most famous blues musicians. Little information is available about his early life, but he probably travelled a lot, moving from town to town playing for tips in local barbershops or restaurants. He was probably a very friendly and outgoing person, creating relationships in communities where he played that served him well when he would pass through the town again in later months. In 1936 and 1937, Johnson recorded more than 25 songs including *Cross Road Blues, Kindhearted Woman Blues, Love in Vain* and the classic *Sweet Home Chicago*. In 1990, the original recordings made by Johnson were compiled into a 2-CD set that won a Grammy Award that year for Best Historical Recording.

Listen to the structure of the lyrics in the music example *Sweet Home Chicago* by Robert Johnson.

Sweet Home Chicago

Come on, baby don't you want to go…

Come on, baby don't you want to go…

Back from the land of California, sweet home Chicago.

Robert Johnson's influence on the blues is still felt today. Eric Clapton has described Johnson's music as "the most powerful cry…you can find in the human voice." Clapton also said that Johnson was "the most important blues singer who ever lived." Other musicians who have admired Robert Johnson include Keith Richards (of the Rolling Stones), Jimi Hendrix, Bob Dylan and Muddy Waters.

W.C. Handy

W.C. Handy (left) and sheet music for *Memphis Blues* (right)

William Christopher Handy (1873–1958) is often referred to as the "Father of the Blues". He was a well-educated musician who made his living as a young man playing cornet (a type of trumpet) in traveling bands. He eventually took a teaching position at a Negro college in Alabama in 1900. He was discouraged that the college considered African-American music inferior to European "classical" music, so he decided to begin touring with a minstrel group again. It was during this time that Handy was exposed to a wide variety of "native" music, spirituals and what would eventually be called "blues".

In 1912, his piece called *Memphis Blues* was published as sheet music and introduced the 12-bar blues form to thousands of people.

Memphis Blues

Handy became a prolific composer of blues music, and achieved success in music publishing. Some of his most famous songs are *Aunt Hagar's Blues* and *Saint Louis Blues.* These songs have been recorded by hundreds of instrumentalists and singers, and continue to be a vital part of the history of music in America.

In 1925, one of the most famous singers of the time, Bessie Smith, recorded *Saint Louis Blues* with another well-known musician of the time, Louis Armstrong. This recording is considered by many music scholars to be one of the finest recordings of blues music of all time. Fantastic video footage of this recording is available at www.youtube.com. Just search *Saint Louis Blues.*

Gospel Music

Around the same time that the secular music called blues was emerging, another style of music called "gospel" was developing. Thomas Dorsey (1899–1993) was a musician and composer who spent much of his early life working as a blues piano player in bars around Atlanta, Georgia. In the 1930s, personal tragedies lead him to sacred music. The new style of music that grew out of this period of his life combined Christian praise—stories of hope and affirmation—with the harmony and syncopated rhythms of blues. The first gospel song ever published was his *If You See My Savior, Tell Him That You Saw Me.*

Dorsey's best known work, and perhaps the most famous gospel song ever, is *Take My Hand, Precious Lord,* which was published in 1932, shortly after the tragic death of his wife and son. Other gospel songs composed by Thomas Dorsey include, *Peace in the Valley*, which he wrote for Mahalia Jackson in 1937, and *If We Ever Needed the Lord Before.*

Mahalia Jackson

Mahalia Jackson (1911–1972) is generally regarded as the finest gospel singer. She was born and grew up in New Orleans, Louisiana. When she was 16, she moved to Chicago where she worked as a maid. It didn't take long for her to find work as a soloist at churches in the Chicago area though, which is where she met Thomas Dorsey. The pair toured small churches for five years, spreading gospel music across the country. Their success helped Mahalia gain enough recognition to get a recording contract with Apollo Records in 1946.

From the mid-1950s until her death in 1972, Jackson was very active in the Civil Rights movement. She was close friends with Martin Luther King Jr., and often performed at his rallies.

Take My Hand, Precious Lord

Through the years, gospel music has continued to grow and thrive. The style has continued to evolve, but the spiritual message of hope and salvation remain a central part of the music. Gospel music today often uses large choirs, multiple soloists, piano, organ, bass, guitar, drums and "horn sections" with trumpet, trombones and saxophones.

Chapter 2: Jazz

Dixieland (1920s)

Spirituals, the blues and gospel are all mainly vocal styles of music. In the early 1900s in New Orleans, Louisiana, a new instrumental kind of music was developing. Dixieland Jazz is a combination of blues and ragtime music along with traditional “brass band” music. Dixieland groups typically have 6–8 musicians and include a “front line” of trumpet, trombone and clarinet. The trumpet usually carries the melody with the trombone and clarinet improvising in the background. The “second line” of Dixieland is usually piano (or guitar/banjo), string bass or tuba and drum set.

Early Dixieland jazz spread to other parts of the country as musicians from New Orleans performed on riverboats that traveled up and down the Mississippi River. St. Louis, Chicago and Kansas City all became important centers for jazz during the 1920s. This example of Dixieland music is a piece called *Washington and Lee Swing*.

Washington and Lee Swing

Paul Whiteman and his Orchestra, 1921.

Louis Armstrong

Please note: Louis Armstrong (Dixieland) and Miles Davis (Jazz-rock) are both identified with several other styles as well as ones used as examples in this book. Armstrong helped move Dixieland toward the "Swing" Era, and Davis was an important figure in swing, bebop and "cool" music along with being an innovator in the jazz-rock style.

Louis Armstrong

One of the greatest jazz musicians of all time began his career playing Dixieland music in New Orleans. Trumpet player and singer Louis "Satchmo" Armstrong (1901–1971) was playing professionally by age 16 and his style of playing and improvising has inspired hundreds of musicians from the 1920s through today. For example, people from Elvis Presley to trumpet great Wynton Marsalis often mention the influence Armstrong's playing and singing had on their own performance.

Some of the most important recordings Armstrong made during his life include *Saint Louis Blues* (the W.C. Handy composition) with singer Bessie Smith and The Hot Five and Hot Seven recordings he made in 1927 and 1928. A piece called *Potato Head Blues* from the Hot Seven record demonstrates Armstrong's sure sense of time and rhythm as he improvises over a long section of "stop time." Listen to the music example to hear how "stop time" sounds.

Potato Head Blues

CD #15

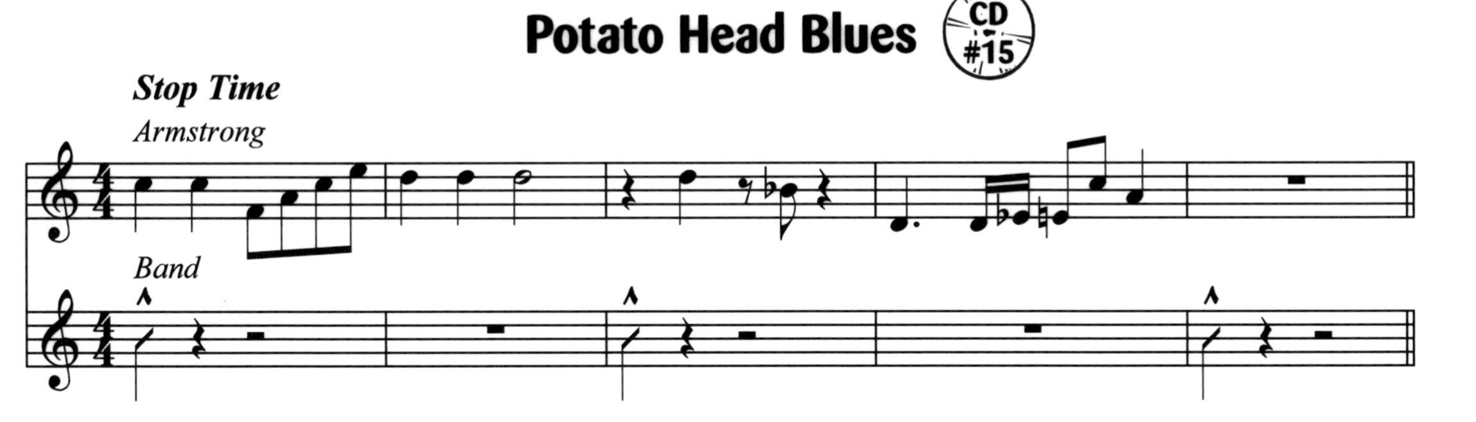

Another noteworthy Armstrong recording was the 1963 hit *Hello, Dolly*. This record became a number one single, and knocked the Beatles off the top of the rankings that year. In 1968, *What a Wonderful World* was another number one hit for Armstrong.

Few people in music history have had the impact on their genre that Louis Armstrong had. He provided the culmination of the Dixieland era and helped pave the way for the next generation of jazz musicians.

Big Band Swing (1930–1940s)

During the years of the Great Depression in America, and continuing through the next decade, *big bands* became popular. These ensembles had 12–18 musicians and the focus of the music shifted away from the free, improvised nature of Dixieland to a style that featured written out "arrangements." These big bands were broken down into sections of saxophones, trumpets and trombones with a rhythm section of piano, string bass and drum set.

Not In the Mood CD #16

Many of the leaders of these bands, as well as some of the players, became famous because they were featured on live, nationwide radio broadcasts each week. Also, the record industry was taking off and sales of big band records skyrocketed. Some of the important band leaders of this era include:

- Benny Goodman
- Tommy Dorsey
- Glenn Miller
- Count Basie
- Artie Shaw

Each of these musicians led bands that played in the largest and most beautiful dance halls in America, and people would come by the thousands to dance and hear them play. One of the crowning achievements of the big band era was a concert performed by Benny Goodman's band at New York City's legendary Carnegie Hall in 1938. Carnegie Hall was (and still is) a highly respected concert setting, so having a "non-classical" performance there was unusual. The success of Benny Goodman's performance there helped win respect and admiration for jazz as a "legitimate" art form.

Count Basie Glenn Miller Tommy Dorsey Benny Goodman Artie Shaw

Duke Ellington

Pianist Edward "Duke" Ellington (1899–1974) is considered to be one of the finest jazz composers. He was also a famous band leader during the big band swing era. He started playing professionally in his hometown of Washington, D.C. and in 1923, he moved to New York. A year later he formed his own band and in 1927, his group was hired to play in Harlem's landmark Cotton Club, where they performed for five years. During this time, Ellington and his band attracted national attention through radio broadcasts and record sales.

Duke Ellington

Ellington was a prolific composer, writing over 2,000 pieces. He had enormous impact on the music of the time and many of his works have become standards in jazz repertoire. Compositions such as *It Don't Mean a Thing If It Ain't Got That Swing, Sophisticated Lady, In a Sentimental Mood,* and *I Got It Bad and That Ain't Good* have been recorded by hundreds of musicians and are known throughout the world. He wrote and arranged most of the music his band played, and because the musicians in his band had all played with him for years, he knew each person's strengths and weaknesses, and wrote the music specifically for each player in his band. Listen to his composition *In a Mellow Tone.*

In a Mellow Tone

During his lifetime, Duke Ellington was nominated for a Pulitzer Prize, elected to the National Institute of Arts and Letters, and was awarded an honorary doctor of music degree from Yale University. In 1969, he was presented with the Presidential Medal of Freedom, our nation's highest honor for a civilian.

Bebop (1945–1960)

In the 1940s, some young musicians were becoming frustrated with the lack of solo opportunities presented in the arrangements of the big bands and were anxious to try new ideas and find new directions for jazz. They were also disillusioned with the idea that jazz was just "dance" music, and were committed to finding a way to show the world that jazz was art music and deserved the same respect given to classical music.

New York City was at the heart of the development of bebop. Characteristics of this style include ensembles of 4–6 musicians, fast tempos and difficult melodies. The compositions performed by bebop players are often called "head charts" because the musicians memorized the melody and chords to each song and would just improvise the introduction, solos and ending. Listen to this bebop piece called *Birds of a Feather*.

Birds of a Feather

During the late 1940s, the popularity of big bands began to decline and bebop was on the rise. Aside from the music itself, there were three other factors that helped fuel the growing interest in bebop:

1. The United States was involved in World War II, and many musicians from bands were drafted (or volunteered) for military service. This made it difficult for leaders to find qualified musicians, so fewer concerts and dances were held.

2. An "entertainment tax" was imposed on dance halls which made it difficult for the owners to stay in business. So, even if a band leader could find enough good musicians, there were fewer places to play.

3. The musician's union ordered a strike against recording studios from 1942–1944, so no new big band music was recording during those years and record sales plummeted.

Sculpture of Charlie Parker by Robert Graham, 1999

Charlie Parker

It would be difficult to overstate the importance of Charlie Parker (1920–1955) in the development of bebop and in the overall growth of jazz as an art form.

Like most jazz musicians of the time, Parker, nick-named "Bird", received the majority of his musical training listening to other musicians play in nightclubs and practicing on his own. He grew up in Kansas City, Missouri and played with several bands. In the late 1930s, Parker moved to New York City and met several important, "cutting edge" musicians like pianist Art Tatum, composer Todd Dameron and trumpet player Dizzy Gillespie. It was here that "Bird" developed his own style of playing. Instead of improvising with just "regular" notes of the chord, he used higher notes of the scale. For example, imagine a musical scale as a ladder with 12 steps. While other players focused on the first, third and fifth steps during their solos, Parker started using the ninth, eleventh and thirteenth steps. He also used long strings of notes in his compositions and improvising. It was a whole new sound!

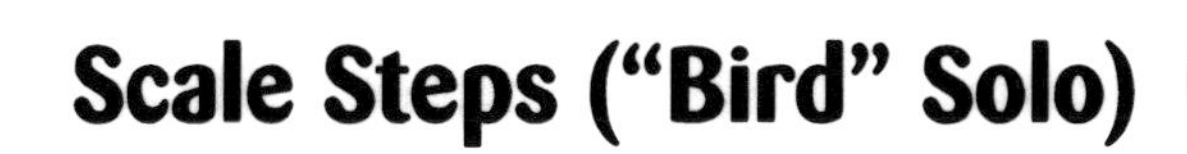

"Bird" note choices

Dizzy Gillespie

John "Dizzy" Gillespie (1917–1993) was a trumpet player, composer and bandleader who worked extensively with Charlie Parker and other musicians in New York City developing the language of bebop. He had a very friendly, outgoing personality and served as a mentor for many young musicians. One of his best known protégés would turn out to be an iconic figure in jazz himself: Miles Davis.

Gillespie's personality also had a lot to do with the gradual acceptance of bebop in the mainstream culture of America. In the 1980s, he led the "United Nations Orchestra", a jazz group that toured Europe and the Soviet Union. He also had numerous guest appearances on television shows including *The Cosby Show, Sesame Street* and *The Muppet Show.* Dizzy's horn-rimmed glasses, beret and goatee soon became symbols of bebop and the "hip" style that became popular in the United States.

Several of Dizzy's compositions have become standards in jazz repertoire. These include: *A Night in Tunisia, Groovin' High*, and *Salt Peanuts.*

Carl Van Vechten

Dizzy Gillespie in 1955

Bird's in Flight

Nelson

Jazz-Rock

Developed in the United States during the 1970s and '80s, jazz-rock (sometimes called "fusion") combined the improvisational, melodic and harmonic components of jazz with the rhythmic drive and electronic instrumentation of rock. Electric guitar, electric bass and all kinds of keyboards and synthesizers are common instruments in jazz-rock, along with acoustic instruments like saxophone and trumpet. Listen to this example of jazz-rock called *City Streets.*

City Streets

CD #21

While bebop was a move away from the more structured music arrangements of the big bands of the 30s and 40s, part of the appeal of jazz-rock was that it was more group oriented than bebop, so longer, more structured forms could be used in addition to improvised sections that featured a soloist. So, instead of a bebop "head chart" that would consist of a 32 measure song repeated several times for solos, a jazz-rock composition might be 60, 70 or 100 bars long and weave sections of improvisation in and out of "written-out" passages.

Two of the important jazz-rock groups that were formed during the 1970s and 80s were *Return to Forever* and *Weather Report*. Pianist Chick Corea was the leader of *Return to Forever*, and this band still records together occasionally. *Weather Report* was co-lead by electric keyboard player Joe Zawinul and saxophonist Wayne Shorter. One of their best selling records was *Heavy Weather*, which featured a piece called *Birdland*. This piece was named for the famous jazz club in New York… "Birdland", named for Charlie Parker.

Miles Davis

Trumpet player Miles Davis (1926–1991) started his career playing in big bands during the 1940s and was an important figure in jazz during the 1950s and 60s. In the mid-1960s, he was one of the first musicians to explore jazz-rock. Over the next twenty years, he recorded many albums that helped shape the course of jazz. He also performed concerts all over the world. He helped many young musicians who played in his groups form their own successful groups. *In a Silent Way*, a jazz-rock album recorded by Miles and his band in 1969 (which included Chick Corea, Joe Zawinul and Wayne Shorter) is viewed by most music scholars as the first successful recording blending jazz and rock styles.

Much like Louis Armstrong, Miles was a seminal figure in the history of American music. Both Armstrong and Davis were tremendous musicians who pushed the limits of one style to the breaking point–so much so that a new style was born. Both were also leaders of successful ensembles that helped launch the careers of dozens of young musicians.

Miles Davis

Louis Armstrong and Miles Davis Comparision

Louis Armstrong	Miles Davis
Instrument: Trumpet	Instrument: Trumpet
Culminator of Dixieland	Culminator of Bebop and "Cool" jazz
Innovator of Swing	Innovator of jazz-rock
Excellent improviser and soloist	Excellent improviser and soloist
Leader of successful ensembles	Leader of successful ensembles

Vistas

Chapter 3: Rock and Roll, Soul, and Hip-hop

Rock and Roll

During the same time that one "branch" of African-American music was growing in swing and bebop, another "branch" developed from the blues and gospel music. Radio show host Alan Freed coined the term "rock and roll" on his show in 1951. He used this phrase to describe music played by one or two electric guitars, bass and drum set that had a heavy *backbeat* (accents on beats 2 and 4). The music almost always featured vocals—usually one of the guitar players was the singer.

From the beginning of rock and roll in the early 1950s there were often stylized dances that were associated with certain songs. A television show called "American Bandstand", hosted by Dick Clark, brought the top rock and roll groups of the day into the homes of hundreds of thousands of teenagers each week, which allowed them to keep up with all the latest dances and fashions.

Chubby Checker was born Ernest Evans in 1941. While joking around during a recording session years later, the name "Chubby Checker" was created, and he has used it since then. In 1961, an appearance on "Bandstand" by Chubby Checker introduced America to one of the biggest dance crazes of all time: the twist.

Before the twist, dance couples were always holding each other. The foxtrot, the tango, the waltz, the polka, the jitterbug and virtually every other popular dance before the 1950s required the partners to move together. The twist allowed each dancer to move by themselves, and that brought all sorts of innovation to the dance floor. Other dance "crazes" of the 1950s that caught the attention of American teenagers were the swim, the jerk, the monkey, the pony, the mashed potato and the watusi.

Johnny B. Goode was another landmark rock and roll song in the 1950s. This was recorded by Chuck Berry (b. 1926) and would end up being one of the most popular songs of all time. John Lennon (of the Beatles) once said that if you wanted to call rock and roll something else, you could call it "Chuck Berry."

Over the years, Berry had a string of Number 1 hits including *Roll Over Beethoven, Rock and Roll Music, Memphis, Tennessee* and *Maybellene.* Many refer to Chuck Berry as the "Father of Rock and Roll."

Chuck Berry

Rock And Roll, Part 1

Johnny Bee

Soul

Soul music is a gritty, vocal style with its roots in gospel, blues and the black church. It reached its peak during the 1950s and 60s, but is still alive and well today. In a National Public Radio broadcast about soul music Ashley Kahn states:

> *Soul [music] often has horn sections and sometimes strings, but it doesn't like to be too dressed up with polished production: soul is more about naked emotion and personal testimony.*

By the 1960s, soul music became part of mainstream American popular culture, and the word "soul" took on a life of its own. There was soul food, soul barbershops, soul handshakes and more. Nelson George, an expert on African-American music and culture wrote: "There was a lot of soul. It was so widely used, it almost lost its meaning." Soul music though, maintained its integrity and continues to be an important part of American music.

James Brown

Often referred to as "The Godfather of Soul", James Brown (1933–2006) was a prominent singer and songwriter from the mid-1950s until his death in 2006. He was especially known for his live performances that featured emotional vocals (including his trademark "shouting") and wild, energetic dancing. Brown had a series of hit singles, including *Please, Please, Please* in 1956, but his first major album was recorded during a performance in 1963 and was called *Live at the Apollo.*

James Brown

A string of hit singles followed this success including:

- *Papa's Got a Brand New Bag (1965)*
- *I Got You (I Feel Good) (1965)*
- *It's a Man's, Man's, Man's World (1966)*
- *Say It Loud—I'm Black and I'm Proud (1968)*
- *Get Up (1970)*

Over the years, hundreds of musicians, including Miles Davis, have cited James Brown as a musical influence.

You Don't Know 

Aretha Franklin

Aretha Franklin (b. 1942) is called "The Queen of Soul". She is listed by Time magazine as one of the 100 most influential entertainers of all time, and was selected to perform at Martin Luther King's funeral and President Clinton's inauguration in 2001, as well as President Obama's inauguration in 2009. She has been an incredibly successful singer, winning seventeen Grammy Awards and having twenty singles reach Number 1. She was also the first woman to be inducted into the Rock and Roll Hall of Fame.

Singers from Whitney Houston to Mariah Carey to Celine Dion have been influenced by Aretha Franklin. Her music typifies the "heart of soul" music. It is edgy, and sometimes raucous. Her singing includes gospel growls and throaty exhortations. Writer Thulani Davis remarked: "Aretha is just more rockin', more earnest, just plain more down front ...she lets her raggedy edges show."

Hip-hop

Hip-hop was born in the early 1970s in the Bronx...one of the five boroughs of New York City. This style of music relies on elaborate sound systems, turntables and a "DJ"—the person who selects the music and runs the turntables—to come to life. It was during the start of the hip-hop style that vinyl records became the standard again because they allowed the DJ to manipulate sounds in ways that were impossible using cassette tapes or CDs.

A DJ, using multiple turntables, took certain percussive sections of songs, called the "break-beats", and played them back-to-back to stretch out the dance portions of these songs. As hip-hop began to evolve, the DJs would add their own comments to the music, giving "shout-outs" to their friends and generally encouraging all the dancers. They also began "scratching"—moving the record on the turntable back and forth quickly to create the distinctive "scratch" sound.** The added vocal parts and other personalization, like scratching, started to move "DJing" to the next level: "MCing". An MC will deliver rhymes and dialog in the rhythm of the music playing. This technique began with street parties thrown by DJ/MC "Kool Herc" in the Bronx in the early 1970s, and was the precursor to rap music.

The popularity of this music gave rise to "break-beat" or "break" dancing. This very stylized, acrobatic and physical movement was embraced by young people all over New York, and has been credited with reducing gang violence.

Kool Herc, Grandmaster Flash and Afrika Bambaataa

These three men are generally credited with starting the hip-hop genre in New York. The techniques they developed are still being used by DJs and MCs today. Some concepts they perfected include:

- Cutting from one record to another without missing a beat
- Playing two records at once and mixing them together
- "Sampling"—recording music or beats from records and mixing them together in new ways
- Using an electronic "beat box" between records

Since its early development in the 1970s, this style of music has become popular worldwide.

Clive "Kool Herc" Campbell (b. 1955) was born in Jamaica and moved with his family to New York when he was twelve. While he was growing up, he listened to Jamacian music along with American music. One of his favorite singers at the time was soul singer James Brown.

Kool Herc

Afrika Bambaataa

In a 1989 interview at The New Music Seminar, Kool Herc describes how hip-hop got started:

My father bought a P.A. system and didn't know how to hook it up...I was messing around with it and I started out by buying a few records to play at my house. When I was doing that I saw a lot of kids playing outside in the backyard. My sister asked me to play at a party and I went out and got around twenty records that I felt were good enough and we gave a party and charged about 25 cents to come in and we made $300.00!

Like Kool Herc, Joseph Saddler (b. 1958), also known as "Grandmaster Flash" grew up in the Bronx. In the late 1970s, Grandmaster Flash formed a group called the Furious Five. *The Adventures of Grandmaster Flash on the Wheels of Steel* was a hip-hop/rap released in1981 that marked the first time that record "scratching" was actually used in a recording. Also interesting to note is that this piece included almost no original material—it was made up of music "sampled" from other recordings.

Afrika Bambaataa (b. 1957) also grew up in the Bronx, and is sometimes called "The Grandfather" of hip-hop. While growing up, Bambaataa was a member of a gang called the Black Spades. He had the opportunity to visit Africa, and when he returned to the United States, he decided to give up the gang life and devote his time to music. In 1983, he and his band, called The Soulsonic Force, released a track called *Planet Rock*. This was one of the first hip-hop/rap pieces that used electronic sounds from a drum machine and synthesizers along with other "sampled" music. The music video for *Planet Rock* featured break dancers, which, for the first time, put national attention on that style of dance.

Conclusions

Hip-hop, soul, rock and roll, jazz, gospel and the blues all have their roots in the black music experience of the plantation songs, work songs and spirituals of the slaves in America during the 1700s. We have seen how everything from the most complicated bebop music to the simply-stated, heartfelt emotions of the blues is part of the tradition of African-American music in the United States.

We have also seen that these art forms often developed side by side—they didn't just appear out of a vacuum. This is true of all art…not just American music. It is important to note that just because a new style of music developed does not mean that previous styles disappeared. Spirituals, jazz, blues and gospel are all alive today. Artists are still recording jazz, spiritual, gospel and blues albums, and new music is being written in these styles every day.

Name ______________________________ Date ______________

Music Lingo

Instructions: Circle the letter of the correct answer for each music review question below.

1. Syncopation is ________________.
   A. Accenting a weak beat in music
   B. The speed of the music
   C. How loud music is
2. A piano could provide ____________ for a solo singer.
   A. Genre
   B. Accompaniment
   C. Solo
3. The speed of a piece of music can be described by its ________________.
   A. solo
   B. chords
   C. tempo
4. A choir with no instrumental accompaniment is singing ________________.
   A. a cappella
   B. solo
   C. classical music
5. ________________ is known as the "Godfather of Soul."
   A. Al Pacino
   B. James Brown
   C. Louis Armstrong
6. Where is the most likely place you would hear an *art song*?
   A. At a recital
   B. On MTV
   C. At the movies
7. ________________ is making up music "on the spot".
   A. Chord
   B. Tempo
   C. Improvisation
8. ______________ is a famous concert hall in New York City.
   A. Carnegie Hall
   B. Times Square
   C. The Bronx
9. Who was the leader of the big band that performed in Harlem's Cotton Club?
   A. Duke Ellington
   B. Benny Goodman
   C. John Philip Sousa
10. A *genre* is ________________.
    A. A particular music composition
    B. A type, class or style of art, music or literature
    C. The solo section of a song
11. A secular song is ________________.
    A. non-religious
    B. soft
    C. very long
12. The "home" of *classical music* is ____________.
    A. America
    B. Japan
    C. Western Europe
13. If music has a heavy backbeat, it has ________.
    A. A fast tempo and a difficult melody
    B. No accompaniment
    C. Accents on beats 2 and 4.
14. A type of religious song written for the purpose of praise, adoration or prayer is a ________________.
    A. Symphony
    B. Jingle
    C. Hymn
15. "Scratching" means to ________________.
    A. Move a record quickly back and forth on a turntable
    B. Play very high notes on a trumpet
    C. Mixing music from various records in new ways

Name ______________________________ Date ______________

Who's Got Style?

Match each of these performers with their music styles.

Fisk Jubilee Singers

Kool Herc

James Brown

Thomas Dorsey

Miles Davis

Louis Armstrong

Robert Johnson

Duke Ellington

Aretha Franklin

Chuck Berry

Charlie Parker

W.C. Handy

Dizzy Gillespie

Chubby Checker

Grandmaster Flash

Style	Artist
Spirituals	
Blues	
Blues	
Gospel	
Dixieland	
Big Band Swing	
Bebop	
Bebop	
Jazz-rock	
Rock and Roll	
Rock and Roll	
Soul	
Soul	
Hip-hop	
Hip-hop	

Name ______________________ Date ______________

Song Styles

Match each of these songs with their music styles.

Song	Style
Deep River	
Memphis Blues	
Take My Hand, Precious Lord	
Washington and Lee Swing	
In a Mellow Tone	
Birds of a Feather	
City Streets	
The Twist	
Johnny B. Goode	
I Got You (I Feel Good)	
Respect	
Wheels of Steel	
Golden Child	

Style Bank
Hip-hop
Soul
Jazz-rock
Rock and Roll
Dixieland
Spiritual
Big Band Swing
Bebop
Blues
Gospel

Name ____ Date ____________________

What Does It Take?

Circle the letter of the correct answer for each question below.

1. To play bebop, you probably need a __________.
   A. saxophone
   B. guitar
   C. choir

2. To play hip-hop, you probably need a __________.
   A. piano
   B. turntable
   C. string bass

3. To play the blues, you probably need __________.
   A. a sound system
   B. a guitar
   C. an orchestra

4. To sing gospel, you probably need a __________.
   A. saxophone
   B. guitar
   C. choir

5. To play Dixieland, you probably need a __________.
   A. trumpet, trombone and clarinet
   B. sound system, guitar and electric bass
   C. synthesizer

6. To play rock and roll, you probably need __________.
   A. a flute
   B. an electric guitar
   C. a violin

7. To play jazz-rock, you probably need __________.
   A. a turntable
   B. an electric bass and synthesizer
   C. a choir

8. To play big band swing, you probably need __________.
   A. saxophones, trombones and trumpets
   B. electric guitars and electric bass
   C. ugly tuxes

Name ______________________ Date ____________

Listening Quiz #1 

Identify the Style

1. ______________________________

2. ______________________________

3. ______________________________

4. ______________________________

5. ______________________________

6. ______________________________

7. ______________________________

8. ______________________________

9. ______________________________

10. ______________________________

Style Bank
Hip-hop
Soul
Jazz-rock
Rock and Roll
Dixieland
Work Song
Spiritual
Big Band Swing
Bebop
Blues
Gospel

Name ______________________ Date ______________

Listening Quiz #2 CD #30

Identify the Style

1. ______________________
2. ______________________
3. ______________________
4. ______________________
5. ______________________
6. ______________________
7. ______________________
8. ______________________
9. ______________________
10. ______________________

Style Bank

Hip-hop

Soul

Jazz-rock

Rock and Roll

Dixieland

Work Song

Spiritual

Big Band Swing

Bebop

Blues

Gospel

Discography

Afrika Bambaataa

Planet Rock: The Album (as part of Afrika Bambaataa & Soulsonic Force), DBK Works, 2005

Looking For the Perfect Beat: 1980-1985, Rhino / ADA, 2001

Louis Armstrong (Dixieland)

Hot Fives and Sevens, JSP Records, 1999

Louis Armstrong: Ken Burns Jazz Collection, Sony, 2000

James Brown

20 All-Time Greatest Hits!, Polydor / UMGD, 1991

Live at the Apollo, Polydor / UMGD, 2004

Chuck Berry

The Definitive Collection, Chess, 2006

The Anthology, MCA, 2000

Chubby Checker

The Best of Chubby Checker 1959-1963, ABKCO, 2005

Miles Davis (Jazz Fusion)

In A Silent Way, Sony, 2002

Miles in the Sky, SBME Special Markets, 2008

Black Beauty: Miles Davis at Filmore West, Sony, 1997

Thomas Dorsey

Precious Lord: The Great Gospel Songs of Thomas A. Dorsey, SBME Special Markets, 2008

Duke Ellington

22 Original Big Band Hits, Hindsight Records, 1994

Greatest Hits, RCA, 1996

Duke Ellington: Ken Burns Jazz Collection, Sony, 2000

Aretha Franklin

The Definitive Soul Collection, Rhino, 2007

Lady Soul, Rhino, 1995

I Never Loved a Man the Way I Love You, Atlantic / WCA, 1995

Dizzy Gillespie (Bebop)

Jazz at Massey Hall (as part of The Quintet), OJC, 1991

Groovin' High, Savoy Jazz, 1993

Town Hall, New York City, June 22, 1945 (live album with Charlie Parker) Uptown Jazz, 2005

Live at the Royal Festival Hall (with the United Nations Orchestra), Red Int. / Red Ink, 2001

W.C. Handy

W.C. Handy's Memphis Blues Band, Memphis Archives, 1994

Louis Armstrong Plays W.C. Handy, SBME Special Markets, 2008

Robert Johnson

The Complete Recordings, Sony, 1996

King of the Delta Blues Singers, Sony, 1998

King of the Delta Blues Singers, Vol. II, Sony, 2004

Grandmaster Flash

The Message (as part of Grandmaster Flash & The Furious Five), DBK Works, 2005

Message From Beat Street: The Best of Grandmaster Flash, Melle Mel & The Furious Five, Rhino / WEA, 1994

Kool Herc

Did not record any albums in his career, but was featured on songs of other artists

Mahalia Jackson

Gospels, Spirituals & Hymns, Sony, 1998

Gospels, Spirituals & Hymns, Vol. 2, Sony, 1998

Charlie Parker (Bebop)

Best of the Complete Savoy & Dial Studio Recordings, Savoy Jazz, 2002

Bird's Best Bop in Verve, Polygram, 2005

Timeless Charlie Parker, Savoy Jazz, 2002

Diz 'N Bird at Carnegie Hall (with Dizzy Gillespie), Blue Note Records, 1997

Spirituals

Fisk Jubilee Singers, Vol. I, Document, 1997

Fisk University Jubilee Singers, *In Bright Mansions*, Curb Records, 2003

Wade in the Water, Vol.1: African American Spirituals: The Concert Tradition, Smithsonian Folkways, 1994

Isaac Watts

When I Survey the Wondrous Cross: Great Hymns of Isaac Watts, Discovery House Music, 2002

PowerPoint Slides

Vocabulary Word Bank

A cappella
Singing without instrumental accompaniment

Accompaniment
A vocal or instrumental part that supports another part

Album
Before CDs, iTunes and mp3 players, music was recorded on vinyl and was referred to as an *album*.

Arrangement
In music, an arrangement means there are specific written parts for each performer.

Art song
A vocal music composition for solo singer and piano intended for a recital or other "formal" performance

Backbeat
When a piece of music is accented on beats 2 and 4

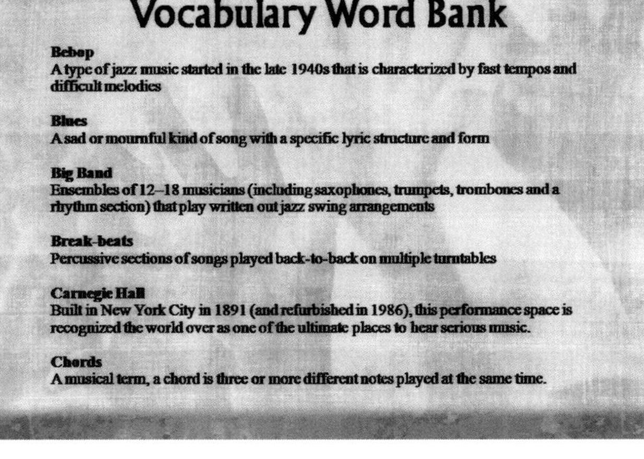

Vocabulary Word Bank

Classical Music
This refers to all "serious" music in the Western European tradition.

Dixieland
A style of jazz, which developed in New Orleans at the beginning of the 20th century

DJ (Deejay or Disc Jockey)
The person who selects music and runs turntables in a dance club

Emancipation Proclamation
This consists of two executive orders issued by President Lincoln during the American Civil War. The first order declared the freedom of all slaves in the Confederate States of America that did not return to the Union by the year 1863. The second order listed the specific states where the proclamation applied.

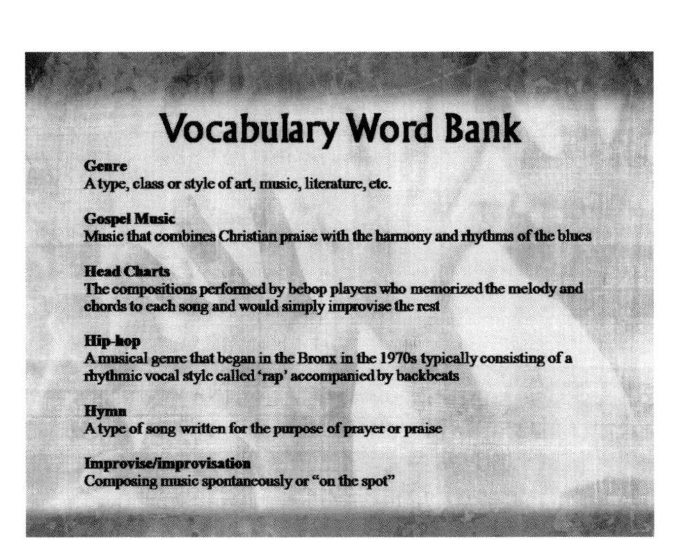

Vocabulary Word Bank

MC (emcee or MJ – microphone jockey)
The host of an event or performance

Measure
A short segment of music

Melody
The most prominent part of a song or instrumental piece

New York City
One of the most important cities in the development of African-American music like jazz and Hip-hop

Ragtime
An American musical genre popular between 1897 and 1918

Repertoire
A collection of music pieces played by an individual musician or group, or composed for a particular instrument or group of instruments

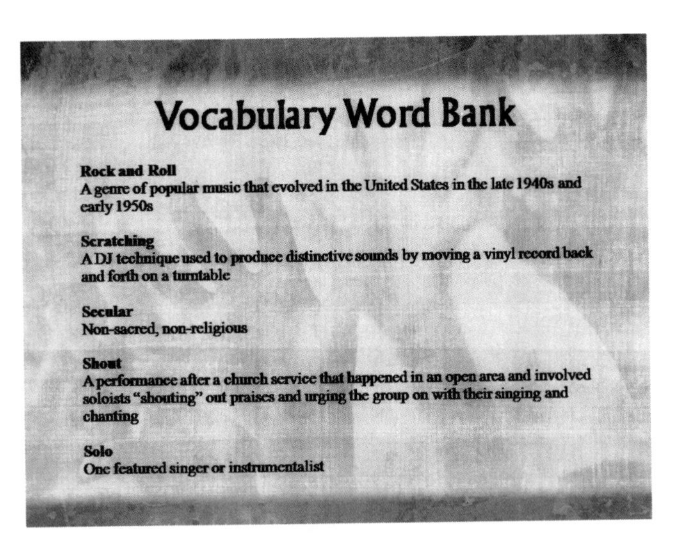
Vocabulary Word Bank
Rock and Roll
A genre of popular music that evolved in the United States in the late 1940s and early 1950s
Scratching
A DJ technique used to produce distinctive sounds by moving a vinyl record back and forth on a turntable
Secular
Non-sacred, non-religious
Shout
A performance after a church service that happened in an open area and involved soloists "shouting" out praises and urging the group on with their singing and chanting
Solo
One featured singer or instrumentalist

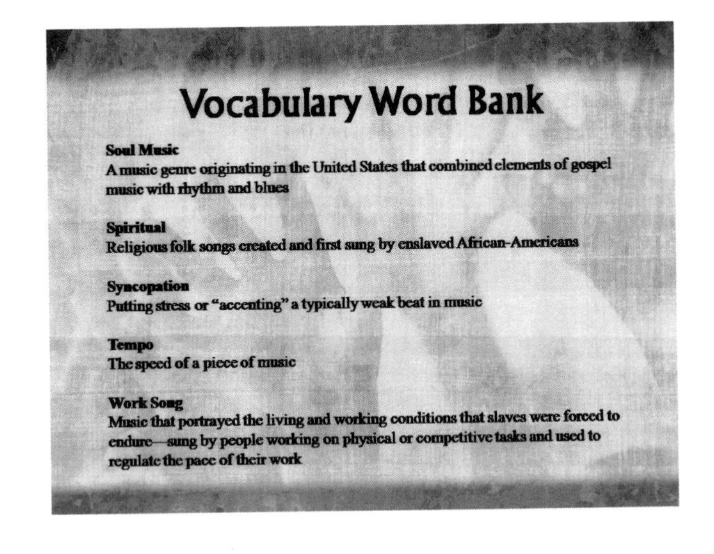
Vocabulary Word Bank
Soul Music
A music genre originating in the United States that combined elements of gospel music with rhythm and blues
Spiritual
Religious folk songs created and first sung by enslaved African-Americans
Syncopation
Putting stress or "accenting" a typically weak beat in music
Tempo
The speed of a piece of music
Work Song
Music that portrayed the living and working conditions that slaves were forced to endure—sung by people working on physical or competitive tasks and used to regulate the pace of their work

A Celebration of Black History Through Music - Styles
1830 1850 1870 1890 1910 1930 1950 1970 1990 2010
Work songs, Hymns, Shouts
Spirituals
Gospel
Blues
Dixieland
Big Band Swing
Bebop
Rock and Roll
Soul
Jazz-rock
Hip-hop
1830 1850 1870 1890 1910 1930 1950 1970 1990 2010

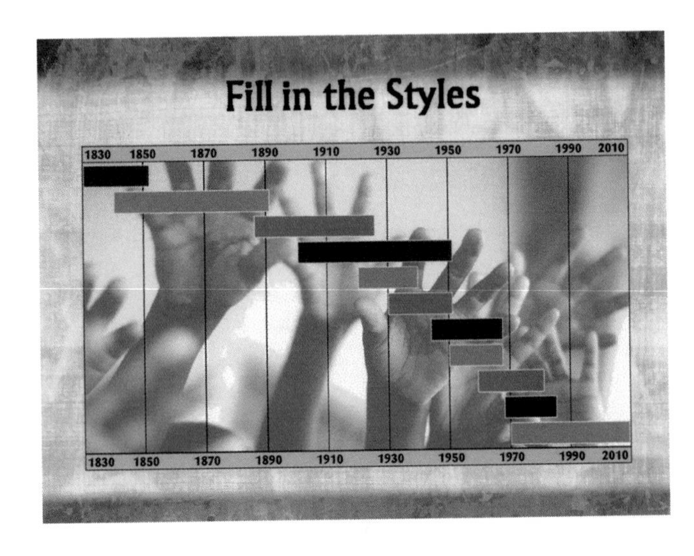
Fill in the Styles
1830 1850 1870 1890 1910 1930 1950 1970 1990 2010
1830 1850 1870 1890 1910 1930 1950 1970 1990 2010

Roots
Work Songs
Hoe Emma, Hoe
Hymns
Shouts
Spirituals
Call and Response
Swing Low, Sweet Chariot
Slow, long-phrased melody
Deep River
Segmented, syncopated melody
Gonna Shout All Over God's Heaven

The Blues
W.C. Handy
Composer:
"Father of the Blues"
Saint Louis Blues
I hate to see the evening sun go down.
I hate to see the evening sun go down.
'Cause my baby, she done left this town.
Robert Johnson
Guitarist/Singer
Gospel Music
Thomas Dorsey
Composer: Take My Hand, Precious Lord
Mahalia Jackson
Gospel singer

Jazz
Dixieland
Louis Armstrong
Potato Head Blues
Big Band Swing
Duke Ellington
In a Mellow Tone
Jazz-Rock
Miles Davis
City Streets
Bebop
Charlie Parker and
Dizzy Gillespie
Birds of a Feather

Rock and Roll
Chubby Checker
The Twist
Chuck Berry
Johnny B. Goode
Soul
Aretha Franklin
"The Queen of Soul"
James Brown
"The Godfather of Soul"

Hip-hop
DJ, sound system, turntables, "scratching"
Grandmaster Flash
Kool Herc
Afrika Bambaataa

Match these
performers with their styles
Kool Herc
James Brown
Thomas Dorsey
Miles Davis
Chubby Checker
Louis Armstrong
Robert Johnson
Duke Ellington
Aretha Franklin
Fisk Jubilee Singers
Charlie Parker
Soul
Blues
Gospel
Dixieland
Spirituals
Bebop
Big Band
Jazz-Rock
Hip-hop
Rock and Roll
Big Band

Match these songs with their styles
Deep River
Memphis Blues
Take My Hand, Precious Lord
The Twist
In a Mellow Tone
Birds of a Feather
Washington and Lee Swing
Johnny B. Goode
I Got You
Golden Child
Soul
Gospel
Blues
Bebop
Rock and Roll
Big Band
Spiritual
Dixieland
Rock and Roll
Hip-hop

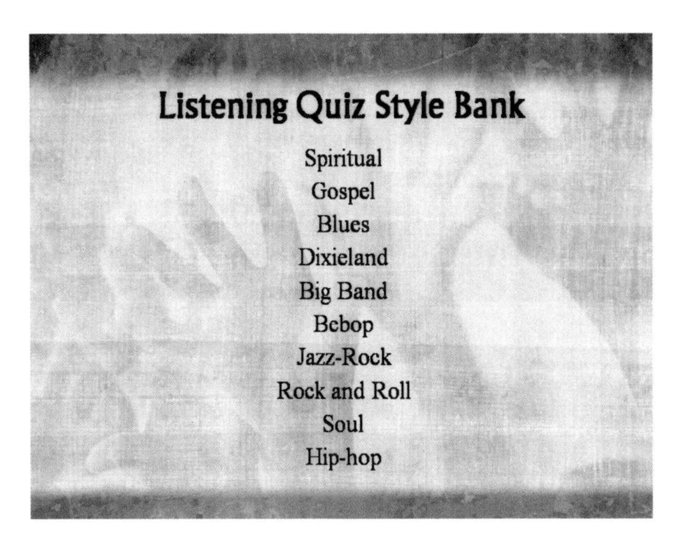
Listening Quiz Style Bank
Spiritual
Gospel
Blues
Dixieland
Big Band
Bebop
Jazz-Rock
Rock and Roll
Soul
Hip-hop

Answer Keys

Music Lingo (pg. 29)

1. A. Accenting a weak beat in music
2. B. Accompaniment
3. C. tempo
4. A. a cappella
5. B. James Brown
6. A. At a recital
7. C. Improvisation
8. A. Carnegie Hall
9. A. Duke Ellington
10. B. A type, class or style of art, music or literature
11. A. non-religious
12. C. Western Europe
13. C. Accents on beats 2 and 4
14. C. Hymn
15. A. Move a record quickly back and forth on a turntable

Who's Got Style? (pg. 30)

Spirituals – Fisk Jubilee Singers

Blues – W.C. Handy

Blues- Robert Johnson

Gospel –Thomas Dorsey

Dixieland – Louis Armstrong

Big Band Swing – Duke Ellington

Bebop – Dizzy Gillespie

Bebop – Charlie Parker

Jazz-rock – Miles Davis

Rock and Roll – Chuck Berry

Rock and Roll – Chubby Checker

Soul – James Brown

Soul –Aretha Franklin

Hip-hop – Kool Herc

Hip-hop – Grandmaster Flash

Song Styles (pg. 31)

Deep River –Spiritual

Memphis Blues – Blues

Take My Hand – Gospel

Washington and Lee Swing – Dixieland

In a Mellow Tone – Big Band Swing

Birds of a Feather – Bebop

City Streets – Jazz-rock

The Twist – Rock and Roll

Johnny B. Goode – Rock and Roll

I Got You (I Feel Good) - Soul

Respect – Soul

Wheels of Steel – Hip-hop

Golden Child – Hip-hop

What Does It Take? (pg. 32)

1. A. saxophone
2. B. turntable
3. B. a guitar
4. C. choir
5. A. trumpet, trombone and clarinet
6. B. an electric guitar
7. B. an electric bass and sythesizer
8. A. saxophones, trombones and trumpets

Listening Quiz #1 (page 33)

1. Soul
2. Rock and Roll
3. Gospel
4. Bebop
5. Spiritual
6. Hip-hop
7. Jazz-rock
8. Blues
9. Dixieland
10. Big Band Swing

Listening Quiz #2 (page 34)

1. Big Band Swing
2. Blues
3. Dixieland
4. Hip-hop
5. Bebop
6. Gospel
7. Jazz-rock
8. Soul
9. Spiritual
10. Rock and Roll